Piano | Vocal | Guitar

Songs of HAWAII

Cover photo courtesy Library of Congress, Prints & Photographs Division
Photograph by Carol M. Highsmith

ISBN 978-1-4950-7618-3

HAL•LEONARD®

7777 W. BLUEMOUND RD. P.O. BOX 13819 MILWAUKEE, WI 53213

Visit Hal Leonard Online at
www.halleonard.com

ALOHA NUI KUU IPO

Words and Music by
ALVIN ISAACS

3

ALOHA OE

Words and Music by
QUEEN LILIUOKALANI

HANALEI MOON

Words and Music by
BOB NELSON

BEAUTIFUL KAHANA

Words by MARY J. MONTANO
Music by CHARLES E. KING

Hawaiian Lyrics

Mau loa no ko'u mahalo nui
I ka nani punono o Kahana.
Ka moani aala anu hea
O na pali a o Koolaulola.
O ka home ia o ka wahine
Puuwai aloha a Inia.
He pua ua milliani ia
E ka malualua kii wai.

O Kalahikiola no ka oi
He puulena ia na ka maka
Kohu kihene pua ka u'i
I luluhe i ka ae o ke kai.
He maile kaluhea ia lai
Haaheo a ke ao naulu.
Ulu ae ka manao he aloha
a kluini pua o Kahana.

BEYOND THE REEF

Words and Music by
JACK PITMAN

Be - yond the reef, _____ where the sea is dark and cold, _____

_____ my love has gone, _____ and our dreams grow old. There'll be no

tears, _____ there'll be no re - gret - ting. _____ Will he re - mem - ber me? _____

BLUE HAWAII

from the Paramount Picture WAIKIKI WEDDING

Words and Music by LEO ROBIN
and RALPH RAINGER

DRIFTING AND DREAMING
(Sweet Paradise)

Words by HAVEN GILLESPIE
Music by EGBERT VAN ALSTYNE,
ERWIN R. SCHMIDT and LOYAL CURTIS

HAWAII PONOI

Words and Music by KING KALAKAUA
and HENRI BERGER

HAWAIIAN LOVE CALL

Written by
IRMGARD F. ALULI

HAWAIIAN WAR CHANT
(Ta-Hu-Wa-Hu-Wai)

English Lyrics by RALPH FREED
Music by JOHNNY NOBLE and LELEIOHAKU

* *Recorded a half step higher.*

HAWAIIAN ROLLER COASTER RIDE

from LILO & STITCH

Words and Music by ALAN SILVESTRI
and MARK KEALI'I HO'OMALU

*Children's Chorus

THE HAWAIIAN WEDDING SONG
(Ke Kali Nei Au)

English Lyrics by AL HOFFMAN and DICK MANNING
Hawaiian Lyrics and Music by CHARLES E. KING

Slowly, with much warmth

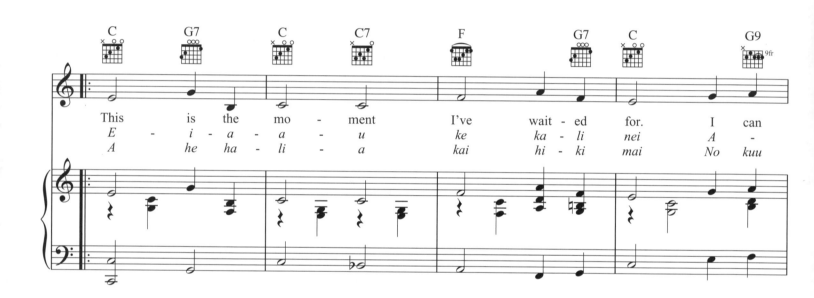

This   is   the   mo - ment   I've   wait - ed   for.   I   can
E -   i - a - a - u   ke   ka - li   nei   A -
A   he   ha - li - a   kai   hi - ki   mai   No   kuu

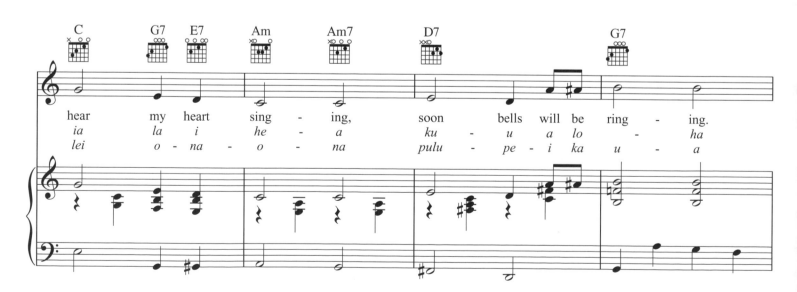

hear   my   heart   sing - ing,   soon   bells   will   be   ring - ing.
ia   la   i   he - a   ku - u   a   lo - ha
lei   o - na - o - na   pulu - pe - i   ka   u - a

I'LL REMEMBER YOU

Words and Music by
KUIOKALANI LEE

HI'ILAWE

Words and Music by
SAM LI'A KALAINAINA SR.

1. Kū-ma-ka ka 'i-ke-na iā Hi -'i-
mai au i ka nu -i
3., 4., 5. *(See additional lyrics)*

la -we ka pa-pa lo-hi mai a-'o Mau-ke-le.
ma -nu Hau wa-la-'au nei pu-ni Wai -pi -'o.

Kū-ma-ka ka 'i-ke-na iā Hi-'i-
Pa-ke-le mai au i ka nu-i

To Coda

la - we ka pa - pa lo - hi mai a - 'ō Ma - u - ke - le.
ma - nu Hau wa - la - 'au nei pu - ni Wai - pi - 'o.

1, 2, 3

4

D(add9)

2. Pa ke-le
3. 'A-'o-le

D.S. al Coda

5. No pu - na

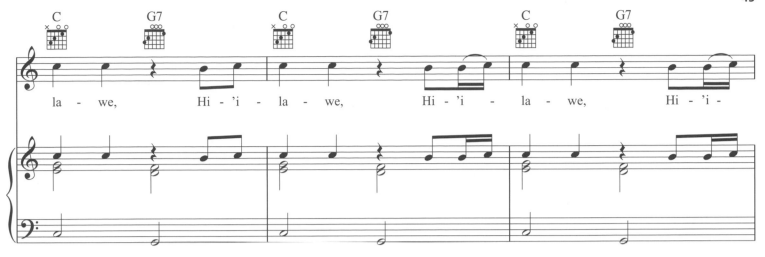

la - we, Hi - 'i - la - we, Hi - 'i - la - we, Hi - 'i -

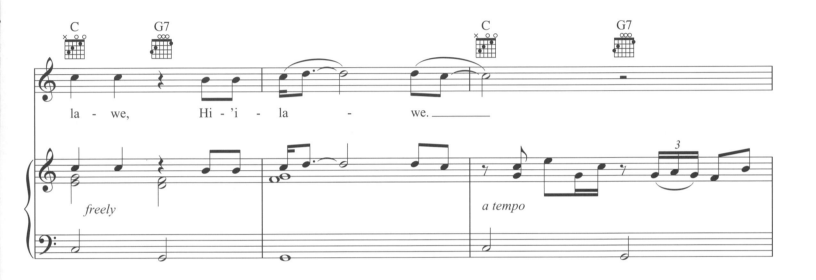

la - we, Hi - 'i - la - we. _____

freely

a tempo

rit.

Verse 3:
'A'ole nō wau e loa'a mai
A he uhiwai au no ke kuahiwi.

Verse 4:
He hiwahiwa au na ka makua
A he lei 'ā 'i na ke kupana.
(To Interlude:)

Verse 5:
No puna ke 'ala i hali 'ia mai
Noho i ka wailele a'o Hi'ilawe.
(To Verse 6:)

English Translation:
All eyes are on Hi'ilawe
And the sparkling lowlands of Maukele.
I escape all the birds
Chattering everywhere in Waipi'o.
I shall not be caught
For I am the mist of the mountains.
I am the darling of the parents
And a garland for the grandparents
From Puna, the fragrance is wafted
To dwell at Hi'ilawe waterfall.
Tell the refrain
All eyes are on Hi'ilawe.

I'LL SEE YOU IN HAWAII

Words and Music by
TONY TODARDO

(There Goes)
KEALOHA

Words by LIKO JOHNSTON
Music by LIKO JOHNSTON and HOWARD ZUENGER

KA-LU-A

Words by ANNE CALDWELL
Music by JEROME KERN

Where the feath-ered palm trees light-ly sway,
Shad-ows fall from ev-'ry haunt-ed pine,

high a-bove the blue Ha-wai-ian
where the moon-rays on the wa-ter

bay,
shine.

set in o-pal,
There's a road of

55

KEEP YOUR EYES ON THE HANDS

Words and Music by TONY TODARO
and MARY JOHNSTON

When-ev-er you're watch-ing a hu-la girl dance, _____ you got-ta be care-ful; you're tempt-ing ro-mance. Don't keep your eyes on her hips, her naugh-ty hu-la hips; just keep your eyes on the hands. Re-mem-ber she's

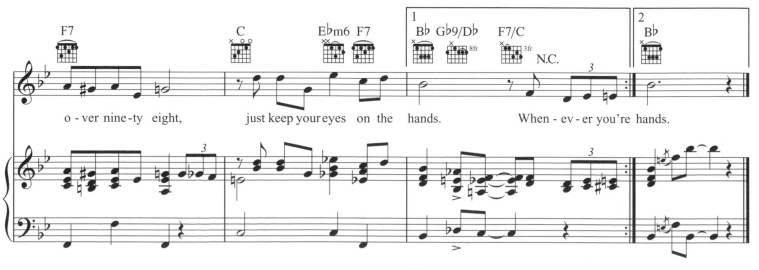

C7

hu - la has a feel - in' that - 'll send your sen - ses reel - in'. It makes a weak man strong. _
grass skirt goes a swish in', keep your head and don't go wish - in' you'd like to mow the lawn. _

F7   **Bb**

Your eyes are re - veal - ing, I'm fool - in' no one; _____ no use in con-

Gdim   **F7**   **Cm7**

ceal - ing we're hav - ing some fun. But if you're too young to date or

F7   **C**   **Ebm6 F7**   **1**   **Bb Gb9/Db F7/C**   **2**   **Bb**
                                              N.C.

o - ver nine-ty eight, just keep your eyes on the hands. When - ev - er you're hands.

LOVELY HULA GIRL

Words and Music by JACK PITMAN
and RANDY ONESS

61

KU-U-I-PO
(Hawaiian Sweetheart)
from SLIVER

Words and Music by LUIGI CREATORE,
GEORGE WEISS and HUGO PERETTI

See the sweet Ha - wai - ian rose, see it blos-som, see it

As the years go pass-ing by, we'll re-call our wed-ding

grow.

day.

That's the sto - ry of our love

I will be there by your side.

ev - er since we said hel - lo.

You will al - ways hear me say:

Ku - u - i - po, I love you

LOVELY HULA HANDS

Words and Music by
R. ALEX ANDERSON

Have you seen the real Ha-wai-ian hu-la, seen the beau-ty of that an-cient dance? Love-ly hands that tell a thrill-ing sto-ry of life and love and gay ro-mance. Love-ly hu-la hands, grace-ful as the birds in mo-tion.

* pronounced "koh-LEE-mah nah-nee eh" (your little fingers)

Bb   D7   Gm

hands.   Ev-'ry lit-tle move ex-press-es   so I'll un-der-stand

C7   Bbmaj7 C7   F6   Dm   F6   Dm Abdim   Gm7   C7

all the ten-der mean-ing   of your hu-la hands,   fin-ger tips that say,   "A - lo - ha." _____

Gm7   C7   Gm7   C7   Bdim   C7

—   Say   to   me   a - gain,   "I   love   you!"   Love-ly   hu - la

1   F   C7   F F#dim Gm7 C7   2   F   C7   F   F6

hands, _ Kou-li - ma na - ni   e.   hands, _ Kou-li - ma na - ni   e.

rit.

MAPUANA

Words and Music by
LANI SANG

MAUI WALTZ

Words and Music by
BOB NELSON

MELE KALIKIMAKA

Words and Music by
R. ALEX ANDERSON

NOW IS THE HOUR
(Maori Farewell Song)

Words and Music by CLEMENT SCOTT,
MAEWA KAITHAW and DOROTHY STEWART

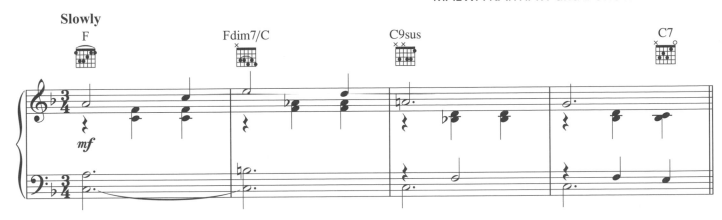

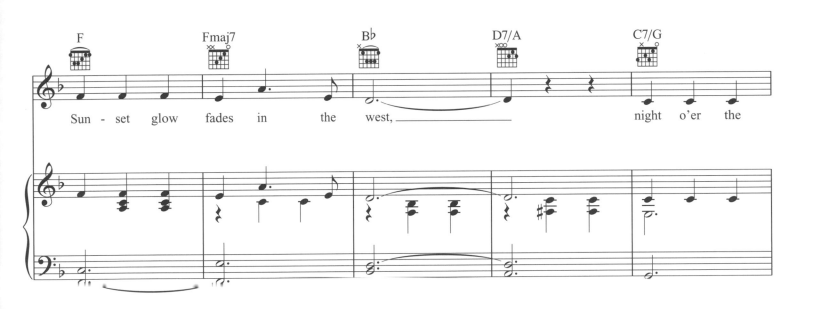

Sun - set glow fades in the west, _____ night o'er the

val - ley is creep - ing! Birds cud - dle down in their

MY LITTLE GRASS SHACK
IN KEALAKEKUA, HAWAI'I

Words and Music by BILL COGSWELL,
TOMMY HARRISON and JOHNNY NOBLE

ON THE BEACH AT WAIKIKI

Words by G.H. STOVER
Music by HENRY KAILIMAIE

"Ho - ni ka - u - a, wi - ki -
"Ho - ni ka - u - a, wi - ki -
"Ho - ni ka - u - a, wi - ki -
"Ho - ni ka - u - a, wi - ki -
"Ho - ni ka - u - a, wi - ki -

wi - ki," sweet brown maid - en said to
wi - ki," she then said and smiled in
wi - ki," she re - peat - ed play - ful -
wi - ki," she was sure - ly teas - ing
wi - ki," you have learned it per - fect -

ONE PADDLE, TWO PADDLE

Words and Music by
KUI LEE

One pad-dle, two pad-dle, three pad-dle for to take me home.

Four-teen on the right, four-teen on the left,

take me to Ha-wai-i nei no-ka best.

To Coda ⊕

OVER THE RAINBOW
from THE WIZARD OF OZ

Music by HAROLD ARLEN
Lyric by E.Y. "YIP" HARBURG

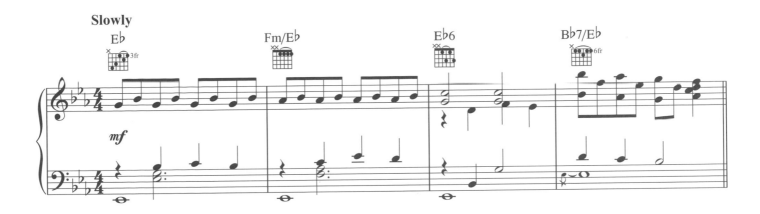

88

OUR LOVE AND ALOHA

Words and Music by
LEOLANI BLAISDELL

PAGAN LOVE SONG

Words and Music by NACIO HERB BROWN
and ARTHUR FREED

PEARLY SHELLS
(Pupu O Ewa)

Words and Music by WEBLEY EDWARDS
and LEON POBER

Pearl-y shells _____ from the o-cean _____ shin-ing in the sun, _____ cov-er-ing the shore. _____ When I see them, _____ my heart tells me that I love you more than all the

SANDS OF WAIKIKI

Words and Music by
JACK PITMAN

SLEEPY LAGOON

Words by JACK LAWRENCE
Music by ERIC COATES

A sleep-y la - goon, a trop-i - cal moon, and two on an is - land, _____ a sleep-y la - goon, and two hearts in tune, in some lull-a-bye - land. _____ The fi - re - flies'

SONG OF THE ISLANDS

Words and Music by
CHARLES E. KING

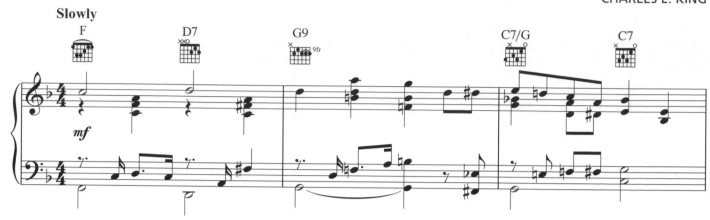

Ha - wai - i isles of beau - ty,_____ where skies are
Na - ni Ha - wa - i - i_____ ka mo - ku

blue and love is true,_____ where balm - y airs and gold - en
o Ke - a._____ Lei ha - a heo i ka le -

SWEET LEILANI
(Lay-la-nee)

Words and Music by
HARRY OWENS

SWEET SOMEONE

Words by GEORGE WAGGNER
Music by BARON KEYES

"T". Al - though you pay no at - ten - tion

to me at all, one kiss and,

need - less to men - tion, I had to fall.

Now I won - der what's keep - ing us a -

THERE'S NO PLACE LIKE HAWAII

Words and Music by
EDDIE BRANDT and TONY TODARO

You can trav - el here and there, you can
heav - en just to be on the

trav - el ev - 'ry - where, but there's no place _____ like Ha -
beach at Wai - ki - ki; oh, there's no place _____ like Ha -

wai - i. _____ It has ev - 'ry - thing and more than you've
wai - i. _____ Girls with flow - ers in their hair and the

TO YOU, SWEETHEART, ALOHA

Words and Music by
HARRY OWENS

TINY BUBBLES

Words and Music by
LEON POBER

Lyrics:

Ti - ny bub - bles ___ (ti - ny bub - bles) in the wine ___ (in the wine) make me hap - py, (make me hap - py), make me feel fine. (make me feel fine.) Ti - ny bub - bles ___ (ti - ny bub - bles) make me warm all

UKULELE LADY

Words by GUS KAHN
Music by RICHARD A. WHITING

WAIKIKI

Words and Music by
ANDY CUMMINGS

YAAKA HULA HICKEY DULA

Words and Music by RAY GOETZ,
JOE YOUNG and PETER WENDLING